D0903096

LIVING WITH DISEASE

HIV/AIDS

BY LORI DITTMER

CREATIVE EDUCATION

Contents

On April 23, 1984, reporters packed a conference room in Washington, D.C., for news about a growing **epidemic** called acquired immune deficiency syndrome (AIDS). There, United States Department of Health and Human Services secretary Margaret Heckler announced that Dr. Robert Gallo had recently pinpointed the virus that caused AIDS. Although his research was still weeks from publication, news of the findings had leaked. Gallo had been pulled away from a meeting in Italy to attend the spontaneous press conference. Anxious and pressed for answers, he told Heckler that a **vaccine** for human testing could be ready in two years. As the years passed without a vaccine, however, Heckler and Gallo were criticized for their optimistic announcement. Researchers had no idea how complex and time-consuming the AIDS puzzle would be to solve. More than 25 years later, there is still no vaccine. However, researchers have come a long way toward understanding AIDS and its underlying cause, now known to be human immunodeficiency virus (HIV).

Margaret Heckler and Robert Gallo's claims regarding the cause of AIDS in 1984 proved to be premature.

FROM APES TO HUMANS

AIDS is a **chronic**, life-threatening

disease caused by HIV. By attacking the immune system, which is the body's source for fighting infections, HIV wears down the strongest of people, making them **susceptible** to a variety of other diseases. Once a person has progressed from HIV to AIDS, he or she will struggle to conquer even the common cold. In many cases, people do not know that they have HIV for many years. After causing a flulike illness shortly following infection, HIV works steadily and slowly for as many as 10 years before a patient notices health problems.

Gay activist groups that formed in the 1970s to seek civil liberties for homosexuals also worked to combat AIDS in the 1980s.

AIDS officially reached the U.S. in 1981, when doctors in New York and California noticed a disturbing pattern of illness. Previously healthy patients were dying from rare diseases, such as severe pneumonia, **tuberculosis** (TB), and Kaposi's sarcoma. The major outbreaks occurred among homosexual men, which led researchers to believe the disease was transmitted through sexual fluids.

Doctors scrambled to find the cause behind this disease. Some thought a fungus caused AIDS. Others believed an underlying illness

weakened the victims' immune systems and allowed other diseases to take hold. In 1983, French virologist Luc Montagnier of the Pasteur Institute identified a **retrovirus** and called it lymphadenopathy-associated virus (LAV). The next year, Gallo, who worked at the National Institutes of Health, determined that the virus, which he called human T-lymphotropic virus type III (HTLV-III), caused AIDS. The two laboratories began working together, and the virus was officially named HIV.

After tracing the disease to Africa, researchers looked back at blood samples that had been kept frozen from previous studies on the continent and retested them for HIV. They found that the virus had been present for many years. The oldest confirmed case was found in a sample taken from a Congolese man in 1959.

Researchers now believe HIV is a **zoonotic** disease; it jumped to humans from chimpanzees and other primates that were infected with simian immunodeficiency virus (SIV). SIV and HIV have a similar **genetic** makeup, and the presence of SIV is widespread among nearly 40 primate species in Africa. Monkeys and chimps were commonly hunted for their meat in the early 1900s. If the person hunting or preparing an infected chimp was cut in the process and chimp blood entered the person's body, so would the virus. Once in the human body,

researchers speculate, SIV changed into a stronger virus that could spread from person to person through bodily fluids. Because there are two types of the virus in humans, HIV-1 and HIV-2, scientists believe there were two separate events when the virus jumped from chimps and monkeys to humans. HIV-1, the more common and harmful strain, has been traced back to chimpanzees. Scientists think that HIV-2 came from the sooty mangabey, a monkey that lives in the forests of West Africa.

Even after HIV began spreading to humans in Africa, doctors likely did not suspect a new illness for many years. TB and diarrhea have long been common problems in Africa, and with medical care in short supply in some regions, physicians probably did not investigate whether a broader cause was behind these illnesses. Then, as global travel increased in the 1970s and 1980s, so did the spread of HIV. Flight attendants, sailors, and other travelers who had come into contact with the disease quickly brought HIV to Europe, Asia, and North America. The 1984 announcement that a vaccine would soon be ready for testing likely helped fuel the spread of HIV as well. Many people who engaged in risky behavior such as unprotected sex believed a cure would save them if they developed the disease, so they did not worry about preventing it.

The common chimpanzee is an endangered species whose populations are expected to continue decreasing.

Although AIDS was referred to as an epidemic in the U.S. in the early 1980s, the general public knew little about the disease and how it spread. Then, celebrities began to reveal that they had it, which increased awareness throughout the country. Actor Rock Hudson was the first major celebrity to publicly announce that he had HIV; he died in 1985. At about the same time, a teenager named Ryan White made headlines for contracting HIV from donated blood products he received to treat his hemophilia (a condition in which the ability of blood to clot, or stop bleeding at a wound, is reduced). Greg Louganis, a former Olympic diver, and basketball great Magic Johnson currently live with HIV.

HIV can be transmitted through blood, bodily fluids during sexual contact, and through a mother to her child via breast milk or at birth. The people at greatest risk for acquiring HIV are those who have regular contact with the bodily fluids of someone who has HIV. Having sex with multiple partners increases the risk of coming into contact with someone carrying the virus. A person who has another sexually transmitted disease (STD) has a higher chance of contracting HIV, because STDs can cause sores through which HIV can enter the body. **Intravenous** drug users who share needles risk acquiring HIV, since the needle touches the blood of more than one person. Until a blood-screening test was

In the U.S., African Americans make up almost half (49 percent) of HIV/AIDS cases. Thirty-one percent of those with HIV/AIDS are white, and 18 percent are Hispanic. Washington, D.C., has the highest prevalence of the disease in the country, with at least 3 percent of residents having either HIV or AIDS.

Ryan White and AIDS Misconceptions

Ryan White was born in 1971 and diagnosed with hemophilia shortly afterward. This disease kept his blood from clotting, so that his body could not stop the bleeding of even the smallest scrape. White depended on **transfusions** of blood-based products to help his blood clot. At the time, tests were not available to screen blood donations for HIV, and in 1984, White discovered that he had received infected blood products after developing a rare type of pneumonia, a telltale sign of AIDS. Because the general public knew little about the disease, people were afraid that White would spread AIDS throughout his school in Kokomo, Indiana. The school banned him from attending, but he challenged the decision in court and won the right to return. In April 1990, at the age of 18, White died. His life inspired the Ryan White Comprehensive AIDS Resources Emergency (CARE) Act, later renamed the Ryan White HIV/AIDS Program, which helps pay for the care of people with HIV.

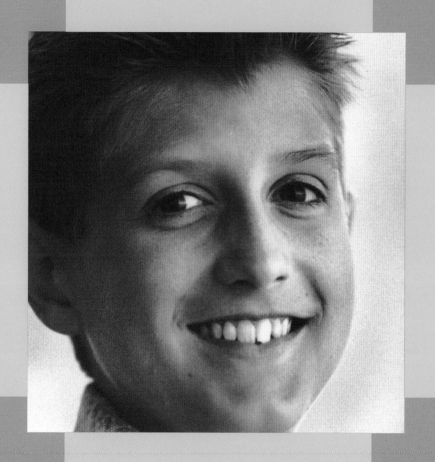

Ryan White's fight to attend school and have a normal childhood, despite having AIDS, gained him celebrity status instead of normalcy.

developed in 1985, the donated blood supply in the U.S. was also at risk. Today, the risk of contracting HIV from donated blood products has been nearly eliminated.

One exposure to HIV does not guarantee transmission. Fortunately, this means HIV is not highly infectious. The disease is not spread through breathing the air, shaking hands, or hugging. There have been no confirmed cases of HIV being contracted from sweat or tears, and although HIV can be present in saliva, the risk of spreading it through kissing is low.

AIDS is now known as a pandemic, or an epidemic that has spread to more than one continent. Recent estimates suggest that 33 million people around the globe are infected with HIV. More than 20 million live in sub-Saharan Africa—the part of the continent south of the Sahara Desert. An estimated 7,400 people around the world become infected with HIV each day. In the U.S., roughly 1 million residents currently live with HIV, and more than 500,000 Americans have died from AIDS since the disease first made headlines in 1981. In 2007, more than 37,000 U.S. citizens were diagnosed with AIDS, while an estimated 14,500 died from the disease that year.

In 2008, 67 percent of HIV/AIDS cases were in sub-Saharan Africa, where 22.4 million people were infected. In Asia, roughly 4.7 million people had the disease, while there were 2 million patients in Latin America, 2.3 million in Europe, and 1.4 million in North America.

CHAPTER TWO

DESTROYING THE IMMUNE SYSTEM

HIV is a retrovirus that can be

further classified as belonging to the genus *Lentivirus*. Lentiviruses target the immune system and cause slow, progressive diseases. There are five types of lentiviruses, each specific to an animal species. HIV is in the primate lentivirus group because it affects apes, monkeys, and humans—all primates.

Once HIV enters a person's body, it needs a host cell, so it combines with white blood cells called CD4 cells. These cells are an important part of the body's immune system, helping to fight off viral infections. Inside a CD4 cell, HIV incorporates itself into the cell's genetic material and begins to replicate, or copy itself. Over time, the virus can churn out up to 10,000 copies of itself in a single CD4 cell, destroying the cell in the process. When an infected cell comes into contact with a healthy cell, it builds a "bridge" to transfer HIV into the healthy cell. With multiple HIV molecules invading thousands of CD4 cells, billions of copies of HIV can be produced each day, and within just 10 days, the virus can spread to cells in the brain and other major organs.

Computer-generated illustrations show how HIV virus particles can erupt from CD4 cells.

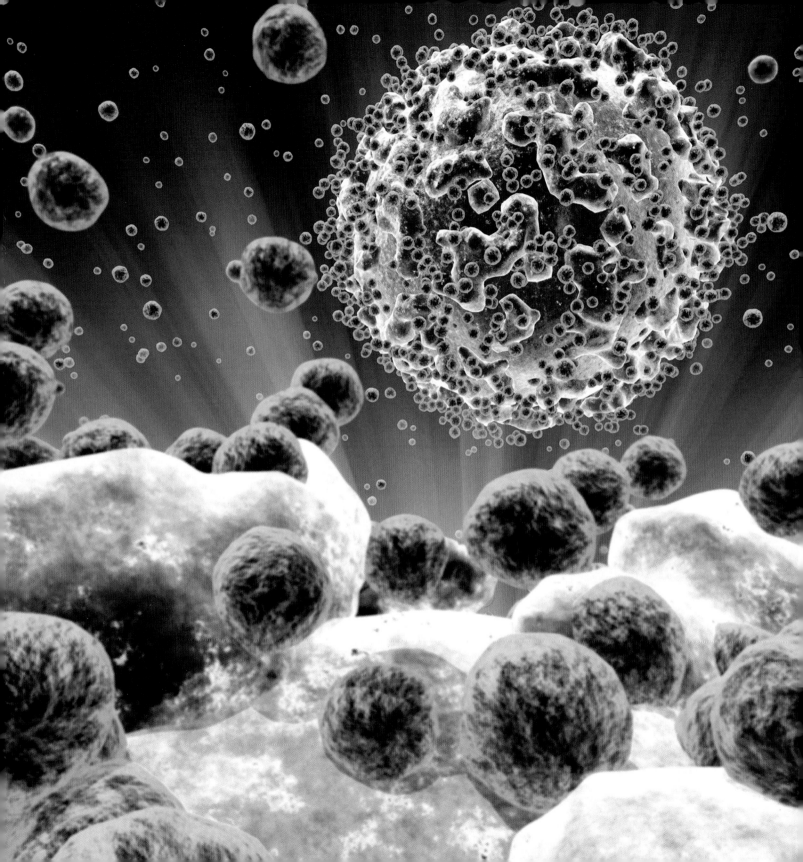

Magic Johnson Contracts HIV

After more than a decade as a legendary point guard for the Los Angeles Lakers, Earvin "Magic" Johnson abruptly announced his retirement from the National Basketball Association in November 1991. Johnson had been tested for HIV as part of a routine screening for a life insurance policy. He was shocked when his doctor informed him that the test had returned positive. Although Johnson's announcement that he had the disease stunned the sports world, it also helped raise awareness of AIDS. He immediately changed his focus from basketball to AIDS research, education, and outreach, creating the Magic Johnson Foundation. With the help of a combination of antiretroviral drugs, Johnson appeared healthy as of 2011. But he stressed that he was not cured and that HIV is a serious condition. "The virus acts different in all of us," he said. "There's no certainty that if you get the virus, you're going to be OK."

Magic Johnson returned to basketball first for the NBA All-Star Game in 1992, then again for part of the 1996 season.

In addition to attacking CD4 cells, HIV can also hide deep in the **lymph nodes**, which are part of the immune system. There, it can remain out of the reach of HIV drug therapies for years before it begins replicating again. As HIV replicates, the virus makes errors, producing copies that are not exactly the same as the original. Consequently, the virus is constantly changing, which explains why so many forms of the disease exist and also makes developing a treatment even more challenging. There are four groups and at least nine subtypes of HIV-1, which are contained in Group M, the most prevalent form of HIV infection. A person infected with one type can also be infected with another. When two different viruses infect the same cell, it's called recombination, which can result in new variations of HIV.

HIV-2 is less widespread throughout the world than HIV-1, and most reported cases of HIV-2 are in Africa. HIV-2 appears to develop more slowly than HIV-1, and those infected with HIV-2 usually survive longer without developing AIDS. People with HIV-2 are also generally less infectious early in the course of the disease, compared with those who have HIV-1. Scientists have not concluded why HIV-2 acts differently, but there are a few possible factors. HIV-2 appears to have a lower viral load than HIV-1, meaning that individuals with the

Seventy-four percent of people with HIV/AIDS in the U.S. are male, because the disease is most prevalent among homosexual men. Worldwide, however, infections are fifty-fifty between men and women. In sub-Saharan Africa, 55 percent of HIV cases are among females.

disease have a smaller amount of the virus in their blood and bodily fluids. HIV-2 might also produce a stronger response from a person's immune system, enabling the body to fight off the virus.

Regardless of whether a person is infected with HIV-1 or HIV-2, after two to four weeks from exposure, the body begins a process called seroconversion, in which the immune system makes **antibodies**. Although the antibodies fight the virus, they can't defeat it completely. Around the time of seroconversion and for up to 3 months after exposure to HIV, between 50 and 90 percent of HIV victims develop flu-like symptoms, including headaches, muscle aches, sore throat, fever, swollen lymph nodes, and sometimes a rash. At seroconversion, a blood test can detect HIV antibodies to determine whether a person has the disease. Those who have HIV are said to be HIV positive.

After seroconversion, most people will not notice symptoms for up to 10 years. Other patients rapidly decline within two to five years. Researchers do not know why some people get sick sooner than others, but they think that the virus progresses faster among those who have a larger amount of the virus in their bodies early on. Also, certain genetic **mutations** might make HIV progress more slowly.

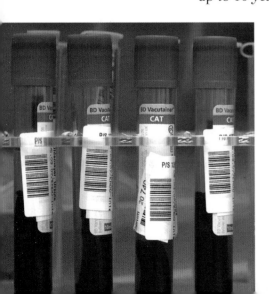

Blood drawn for testing is deposited into small containers called vials.

Even while a person is symptom-free, HIV continues to disable CD4 cells. As their bodies slowly lose these cells, patients' immune systems grow weaker and become unable to fend off other diseases, such as cancer, pneumonia, and influenza. These illnesses, in the presence of HIV, are called opportunistic infections, because a healthy immune system would normally fight them off. Patients receive an official AIDS diagnosis once they test positive for HIV and have either an opportunistic infection or a CD4 count of 200 cells per cubic millimeter of blood (about one drop) or lower. In comparison, a healthy individual has a CD4 level of 800 to 1,200 per cubic millimeter.

Cancer is among the most common opportunistic infections, especially when someone is in the last phase of HIV, diagnosed as AIDS. Cancer affects about 40 percent of HIV/AIDS patients. Kaposi's sarcoma, a rare cancer among otherwise healthy people, is widespread among those with HIV and is likely to appear when CD4 levels drop to 400 or lower. About 20 percent of men with HIV in the U.S. develop this cancer, which is known mostly for causing **lesions** on the skin and mouth. In many **developing nations**, TB and HIV go hand in hand. Not only are those with HIV more susceptible to TB, but once they contract it, TB appears to increase the rate at which HIV copies itself.

BY THE NUMBERS Roughly 22 million people in the U.S. are tested for HIV each year. Nearly one-third of those tested at public testing sites do not go back to get their results. These people are a portion of the estimated 233,000 individuals across the country who do not know they have the disease.

Some HIV victims catch a rare form of pneumonia, called pneumocystis carinii pneumonia. Others suffer from complications such as wasting syndrome, which usually involves diarrhea, weakness, and a 10 percent loss of body weight. If opportunistic infections are not treated, they can kill HIV/AIDS patients.

A small number of HIV/AIDS patients remain free of opportunistic infections without therapy for more than 10 years. While these people seem healthy, they still carry the virus and can spread it to others. However, many in this group don't know they have HIV. Researchers estimate that in the U.S. alone, approximately 233,000 people are infected but are not aware of it.

Still others, just a small percentage of the population, remain HIV negative despite their having been exposed to HIV. These people, who are referred to as "exposed **seronegative**," do not show the virus or measurable antibodies to the disease in their blood. Researchers are trying to figure out why such people are protected from the virus. Their theories range from differences in genetic makeup to an individual immune system's ability to produce different responses according to the viral load of the disease.

CHAPTER THREE

LIVING WITH HIV/AIDS

After more than two decades of research, a treatment to prevent or cure HIV remains elusive. However, many drugs, called antiretrovirals, are available to help prevent the onset of opportunistic infections and delay the development of AIDS. The first drug for this purpose was approved in 1987. It was called azidothymidine, or AZT, and had previously been researched as a cancer treatment.

At first, AZT was prescribed in large doses, but for many people, the benefits of keeping HIV symptoms away came with serious side effects such as muscle weakness and pain, an increased risk of developing bacterial and fungal infections, and **anemia**. Although the dosage was lowered to help reduce side effects, the benefits of AZT were short-lived in most patients, and types of HIV **resistant** to AZT began circulating in their bodies.

Today, roughly 30 drugs are available to treat HIV. There are five major classes of drugs (excluding combined forms). Some prevent HIV from replicating within a cell, while others keep HIV from entering a CD4 cell in the first place. Because the different types of drugs work

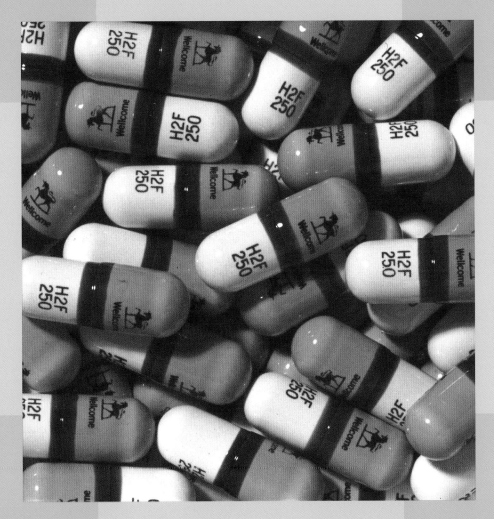

First produced by the Burroughs-Wellcome Company in the mid-1980s, AZT became the AIDS drug of choice.

Before the Epidemic

HIV was recognized as an epidemic in the 1980s as the virus spread through the U.S. However, looking back at blood samples and disease trends, scientists have found that HIV affected other parts of the world years earlier. The earliest documented evidence of HIV was found in a blood sample collected from the African Congo in 1959. Researchers have also discovered evidence that a Norwegian family suffered from HIV in the 1960s, after the father had traveled to Africa. In the 1970s, doctors in Uganda observed a mysterious illness that affected otherwise healthy individuals. Victims of the disease wasted away to skin and bones and suffered from recurring diarrhea, TB, and oral thrush, an infection in the mouth. Locals called the disease "Slim" in reference to patients' malnourished appearance. By the next decade, people in Nairobi were calling the condition "Plastic," because, once victims died, city workers quickly covered them with sheets of plastic and carried them away.

Groups such as KENWA (Kenya Network of Women with AIDS) assist African victims of AIDS, especially women and children.

in different ways, and each on its own does not work as effectively, the medications are prescribed in combinations of twos or threes. Physicians generally recommend that patients begin combination drug therapy once their CD4 level drops to around 350.

Drug combinations do not cure AIDS, but they do fight the HIV virus, allowing a patient's CD4 cell count to grow, which helps reduce and prevent the opportunistic infections of later-stage HIV/AIDS. In some cases, the drugs have worked so well that they brought patients back from near death. This phenomenon is called the "Lazarus effect," which is a reference to the biblical account of Jesus raising a man named Lazarus from the dead. Taken soon enough, combination therapy can also help keep pregnant mothers with HIV from passing it to their babies. As a result of these drugs, during the late 1980s and early 1990s, doctors in the **Western** world, where drugs were readily available, began to consider HIV a chronic yet manageable disease, instead of a **terminal** illness.

Still, challenges remain for people who need these drug "cocktails." Treatment often comes with unpleasant side effects, including allergic rashes, anemia, nausea, vomiting, diarrhea, and disorders of the **pancreas** and kidneys. In addition, combination therapy requires a major commitment, involving as many as 25 pills a day, taken at specific

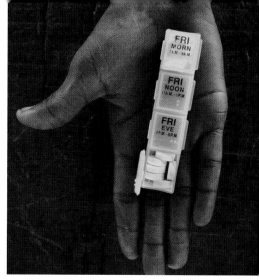

intervals. And no drug combination can reach HIV hidden in body tissues such as the lymph nodes.

HIV can also become resistant to drugs. This is especially likely if patients do not take their medication in the correct doses and at the right times of the day. Once the drugs stop working for someone, the person must switch to a different combination. People who change drugs repeatedly may eventually run out of effective drug combinations. Also, if someone contracts HIV from a person on drug therapy, there is a danger that the newly infected person will develop a mutated form of HIV that is resistant to therapy.

Patients on a combination treatment plan often keep their pills sorted and labeled by day and time.

Combination therapy for HIV is expensive, costing thousands of dollars per year to treat just one patient. As a result, the majority of people with AIDS—particularly those in Africa, Latin America, and Southeast Asia—do not have access to affordable treatments or medications. With financial donations from the world's wealthiest nations, some of these people have received treatment. However, six to seven million people, mostly in sub-Saharan Africa, still lack drug therapy and remain on the fatal path to AIDS.

To stay healthy for as long as possible, individuals with HIV are advised not only to take medication but also to make healthy lifestyle

Washing produce before consuming it may rid it of harmful bacteria or contaminants.

choices. By not smoking, eating nutritious foods, exercising, getting enough sleep, and drinking pure filtered or boiled water, HIV patients can strengthen their bodies against viruses and other opportunistic infections.

HIV-positive individuals also need to avoid bacteria by thoroughly cooking meat, washing fruits and vegetables, and keeping their hands clean. In addition, these individuals should receive vaccinations for opportunistic diseases such as influenza, pneumonia, and **meningitis**, which their weakened immune systems would be unable to fight. Live virus vaccines, such as FluMist (a nasal-spray vaccine for influenza) and the vaccine for chicken pox, generally are not recommended for people with HIV because they involve injecting a person with a weakened form of the virus, and an HIV patient's immune system might not be strong enough to fight the germs that would help a healthy body build up a resistance.

Because HIV is a life-threatening disease, several countries, including the U.S., consider the intentional or reckless transmission of the virus a crime. Those who knowingly infect others or do nothing to prevent themselves from infecting others can be charged with criminal transmission of HIV or even murder, manslaughter, attempted murder,

Nearly 430,000 infants are infected with HIV from their mothers each year. In the African nation of Uganda alone, roughly 30,000 babies are born with HIV annually. Treating HIV-positive women with medication during their pregnancy can reduce the risk that the virus will be passed to their babies from 45 percent to less than 2 percent.

Across the globe, roughly 2.1 million children younger than 15 have AIDS. An estimated 90 percent of these children were infected in the womb, during delivery, or through breastfeeding. In addition, an estimated 14 million children have been orphaned because their parents died from the disease. Researchers expect this number to double in 10 years.

or assault. In 2009, a man from Dallas, Texas, was sentenced to 45 years in prison after intentionally infecting 6 women with the virus.

To help prevent the spread of HIV, people with the disease need to take several precautions. First, these people need to tell their health care providers, family members, and close friends about their HIV status so that everyone involved can use care as they interact. **Abstaining** from sexual activity—with a partner who may not be HIV positive—is the best way to avoid spreading HIV. Consistent use of latex condoms greatly reduces the chance of contracting HIV through sexual activity, too. People with HIV should not share needles, syringes, razor blades, or toothbrushes. They should not donate blood, plasma, or organs.

Fifty-three-year-old Dallas resident Philippe Padieu was charged with aggravated assault for knowingly infecting women with HIV.

People without HIV can stay safe by avoiding contact with another person's blood and bodily fluids. Avoiding alcohol and drugs can also help prevent the spread of HIV. While these substances do not cause HIV, they often lead to risky behaviors, such as unprotected sex or the sharing of needles, because they affect a person's ability to think clearly and make good choices.

CHAPTER FOUR

VACCINE HOPES

After more than 25 years of failure,

hope of finding a vaccine or cure for HIV has faded, yet researchers continue to try. To test drugs that might someday help humans, scientists first use animals. Most AIDS research has involved monkeys and apes. Chimpanzees infected with SIV have been found to develop an AIDS-like illness, and because these apes were possibly the original source of HIV in humans, researchers have been studying them since the 1980s.

Scientists then shifted their focus to captive rhesus macaques, monkeys native to southern Asia, which are regularly used in medical research. Unlike chimpanzees, macaques were plentiful and relatively cheap to obtain. Although macaques do not get sick from HIV-1, they respond to some types of HIV-2 and SIV. They generally develop AIDS and die within a short time after infection.

Recently, macaques have been used in testing to make sure AIDS drugs will be safe for humans. For example, the early HIV drug AZT was first tested on rhesus macaques. More often, though, these monkeys have been used for vaccine tests. The value of animal testing is a

Rhesus macaques are adaptable creatures and easy to take care of, making them attractive to researchers.

controversial topic. SIV does not behave in exactly the same way as HIV does. A drug successful among macaques could fail in humans. Many scientists feel that, in order to learn whether a vaccine will work in humans, it must be tested on humans. However, it would be unethical to give a trial vaccine to people without HIV and then "test" it by infecting them with the virus. So researchers test vaccines on volunteers who live in areas, such as sub-Saharan Africa, where HIV is prevalent. Then scientists track participants to see if they contract the virus during the course of their lives.

Human testing of HIV vaccines involves three phases of clinical trials. Ultimately, scientists are looking for a drug that is safe and long-lasting, protects individuals from infection, and reduces the amount of virus in bodily fluids. During Phase I, a drug is tested on 20 to 100 volunteers who do not have HIV to make sure the drug does not cause harmful side effects. If successful after 12 to 18 months, the drug moves on to Phase II, which involves 100 or more volunteers who are HIV negative but are at high risk for getting the virus, either because of where they live or their lifestyle choices. Over the span of two to three years, researchers figure out if the vaccine works at all and, if so, the quantity of the drug that should be used. Phase III clinical trials are similar to Phase

The First Human HIV Vaccine Trial

While other researchers were testing HIV vaccines on monkeys, Dr. Daniel Zagury, a professor at a French medical university, decided to leap forward and become the first to work with human volunteers. In fact, the first volunteer was Zagury himself. He injected himself with the vaccine he planned to use and, after suffering no ill effects, moved on to others. In November 1986, after working with the government of Zaire in central Africa, Zagury began a trial, starting with two women who had been diagnosed with AIDS. He then included 8 more women and their children, ages 2 to 12 years old. The controversial project stirred up ethical questions, as the study involved healthy children. Zagury claimed that their mothers had begged him to include them in the trials. Although his vaccine appeared to produce an immune response among test subjects, he was criticized for not waiting to see if the drug was first successful in animals.

II but are conducted on a larger scale of several thousand individuals. The HIV-negative volunteers are placed into two groups; one group gets the potential vaccine, while the other gets a placebo, which looks like the medication but contains no active ingredients and offers no protection against HIV. This final phase can take several years, as researchers watch and wait for results and then compare the two groups. If many members of the placebo group develop HIV, while the vaccine group remains largely HIV-negative, the vaccine may be successful.

More than 100 Phase I trials and 20 Phase II trials for HIV vaccines have been completed, are in progress, or are being considered. Few Phase III trials have ever been completed because most drugs do not pass Phase II. In 2009, three vaccines advanced to Phase III testing, and several more were in the works. Much of this research is paid for by the Global HIV Vaccine Enterprise, a collaborative effort including private organizations, such as the Bill and Melinda Gates Foundation, as well as government-sponsored groups such as USAID.

After numerous failed tests to find an effective HIV vaccine, researchers have collected a lot of information about why some vaccines do not work. Because there are many groups and subtypes of HIV, a vaccine created to target one type probably wouldn't work against others. Also,

Philanthropists such as
Bill and Melinda Gates
can use their wealth
to help other people
around the world.

The majority of people with HIV/AIDS in Africa are between the ages of 15 and 49. This has greatly lowered life expectancy in many countries. In 1997, residents of the sub-Saharan country of Swaziland could expect to live to age 60. By 2010, life expectancy had dropped to roughly 48 years.

once HIV infects someone, the virus changes over time as it copies itself, making it hard to target. In addition, unlike previous disease epidemics, HIV directly attacks and damages the immune system, the very powerhouse responsible for fighting infections. This has led many to believe that the creation of a vaccine to prevent HIV is not possible.

In 2009, however, the results of a Phase III study renewed hopes that a vaccine might someday prevent HIV infection. The U.S. Military HIV Research Program sponsored a study of more than 16,000 volunteers in Thailand. The volunteers were all between the ages of 18 and 30 and were at various levels of risk of becoming infected with HIV. For the first time, scientists used a combination of vaccines, similar to the "cocktail" method used to treat HIV infections. Half of the volunteers received the vaccine, while the other half took a placebo. After 3 years, 74 people in the placebo group contracted HIV, compared with 51 participants in the vaccine group.

Despite the modest results, this was the first study to suggest that some people received protection from a vaccine—vaccine recipients were 31 percent less likely to become infected. However, because the study targeted HIV subtypes common in Thailand, scientists do not

Although vaccines exist for many diseases once deemed terminal, scientists have yet to discover one for AIDS.

know how the potential vaccine will affect other types of the disease. They continue to monitor study participants in order to determine how long the protection will last and whether individuals will need booster shots to keep up their immunity.

The small success of one study does not mean that AIDS is about to be eliminated. A vaccine for the public could be many years away. But after examining the results of the Thai study, Dr. Anthony Fauci, director of the National Institute of Allergy and Infectious Diseases, said that it was "an important step forward in HIV vaccine research." Still, the best weapon against HIV remains preventing it by avoiding the risky behaviors that can lead to the disease.

From December 2003 to December 2005, the World Health Organization helped increase the number of low- and middle-income HIV/AIDS patients receiving antiretroviral medication from 400,000 to 1.3 million. Although 4 million people in developing nations now receive antiretrovirals, that number represents only 42 percent of those who need the drugs.

GLOSSARY

abstaining: refraining from something by one's own choice

anemia: a shortage of red blood cells that can lead to extreme fatigue and trouble concentrating

antibodies: proteins in the blood that are produced in response to a bacteria or virus and help fight a disease

chronic: lasting a long time or constantly recurring

controversial: causing a dispute between two sides with opposing views

developing nations: the poorest countries of the world, which are generally characterized by a lack of health care, nutrition, education, and industry; most developing countries are in Africa, Asia, and Latin America

epidemic: a disease that has spread rapidly through a segment of the population in a given geographic area

genetic: having to do with the genes, the basic units of instruction in a cell, which control a person's physical traits and pass characteristics from parents to offspring

intravenous: injected into a vein

lesions: visible abnormalities of the skin, such as wounds, sores, rashes, or boils

lymph nodes: small, circular organs that supply white blood cells to the bloodstream and remove bacteria and foreign particles from tissues

meningitis: a serious inflammation of the membranes covering the brain and spinal cord

mutations: changes in genetic material that are relatively permanent, resulting in a new characteristic or cell function

pancreas: a large gland near the intestines that aids in digestion and produces a hormone called insulin

resistant: unaffected by the harmful effects of something, such as a drug

retrovirus: a virus that incorporates itself into the genetic material of a cell and copies itself, preventing the cell from carrying out its natural function and turning it into a factory to make new viruses

seronegative: having no detectable antibodies (disease-fighting proteins) against a specific disease

susceptible: likely to be affected

terminal: ending in death

transfusions: transfers of donated whole blood or blood products, such as red blood cells, plasma, or platelets, into a blood vessel

tuberculosis: an infectious disease that usually affects the lungs

vaccine: a substance given in a shot or by mouth that helps the immune system form antibodies (disease-fighting proteins) to fight off a specific disease

Western: having to do with the western part of the world, particularly Europe and North America

zoonotic: describing a disease that can be transferred from animals to people

BIBLIOGRAPHY

Cohen, Jon. *Shots in the Dark: The Wayward Search for an AIDS Vaccine.* New York: W. W. Norton & Company, 2001.

Levy, Jay. *HIV and the Pathogenesis of AIDS.* Washington, D.C.: ASM Press, 2007.

Marchione, Marilynn. "In a First, an AIDS Vaccine Shows Some Success." *Yahoo News*, September 24, 2009. http://news.yahoo.com/.

Mayo Clinic Staff. "HIV/AIDS." Mayo Foundation for Medical Education and Research. http://mayoclinic .com/health/hiv-aids/ds00005.

National Center for HIV/AIDS, Viral Hepatitis, and TB Prevention. "HIV and AIDS in the United States: A Picture of Today's Epidemic." Centers for Disease Control and Prevention. http://www.cdc.gov/hiv/ topics/surveillance/united_states.htm.

Nolen, Stephanie. *28: Stories of AIDS in Africa.* New York: Walker & Company, 2007.

Sternberg, Steve. "Magic Johnson Combats AIDS Misconceptions." *USA Today*, December 1, 2006.

Williams, Mary, ed. *Epidemics: Opposing Viewpoints.* Farmington Hills, Mich.: Greenhaven Press, 2005.

FURTHER READING

Aldridge, Susan. *AIDS.* Mankato, Minn.: NewForest Press, 2011.

Bush, Jenna. *Ana's Story: A Journey of Hope.* New York: HarperCollins, 2007.

Hinds, Maurene. *Fighting the AIDS and HIV Epidemic: A Global Battle.* Berkeley Heights, N.J.: Enslow, 2008.

James, Otto. *AIDS.* North Mankato, Minn.: Smart Apple Media, 2009.

INDEX

Published by Creative Education • P.O. Box 227, Mankato, Minnesota 56002
Creative Education is an imprint of The Creative Company
www.thecreativecompany.us
Design and production by The Design Lab • Art direction by Rita Marshall
Printed by Corporate Graphics in the United States of America
Photographs by Alamy (Olaf Doering, Chris Howarth/Australia, Peter Arnold, Inc., Picture Contact), AP Images (Lana Harris), Corbis (Naashon Zalk), Getty Images (Wolfgang Bayer, Stephen Dunn/Allsport, Incredible Features/Barcroft Media, Peter Keegan/Authenticated News, SSPL, Brent Stirton, Taro Yamasaki/Time & Life Pictures), iStockphoto (Christopher Craig, Svengine)
Copyright © 2012 Creative Education
International copyright reserved in all countries. No part of this book may be reproduced in any form without written permission from the publisher.
Library of Congress Cataloging-in-Publication Data
Dittmer, Lori. HIV/AIDS / by Lori Dittmer. p. cm. — (Living with disease)
Includes bibliographical references and index. Summary: A look at HIV/AIDS, examining the ways in which the disease can be contracted, its symptoms and diagnosis, the effects it has on a person's daily life, and ongoing efforts to find a cure.
ISBN 978-1-60818-071-4
1. AIDS (Disease)—Juvenile literature. I. Title. II. Series.
RC606.65.D58 2011   616.97'92—dc22   2010030234

CPSIA: 110310 PO1384
First Edition 9 8 7 6 5 4 3 2 1